Pebble®

Our Community Helpers

Construction Workers Help

by Tami Deedrick

Consulting Editor: Gail Saunders-Smith, PhD

CAPSTONE PRESS
a capstone imprint

Pebble Books are published by Capstone Press,
1710 Roe Crest Drive, North Mankato, Minnesota 56003
www.capstonepub.com

Library of Congress Cataloging-in-Publication Data
Cataloging-in-Publication information is on file with the Library of Congress.
ISBN 978-1-4765-3950-8 (library binding)
ISBN 978-1-4765-5154-8 (paperback)
ISBN 978-1-4765-6011-3 (ebook PDF)

Note to Parents and Teachers

The Our Community Helpers set supports national social studies
standards for how groups and institutions work to meet individual
needs. This book describes and illustrates construction workers.
The images support early readers in understanding the text. The
repetition of words and phrases helps early readers learn new
words. This book also introduces early readers to subject-specific
vocabulary words, which are defined in the Glossary section. Early
readers may need assistance to read some words and to use the
Table of Contents, Glossary, Read More, Internet Sites, and Index
sections of the book.

Printed in the United States of America in North Mankato, Minnesota.
092013   007764CGS14

Table of Contents

What Is a Construction Worker?

Construction workers are people who build things. They build homes, schools, and skyscrapers. They also build roads and bridges.

What Construction Workers Do

Construction workers dig, pound, cut, and measure. They follow plans drawn by architects or engineers.

Construction workers work on job sites. They work together in crews. Everyone has a job to do. Framers build walls. Roofers nail shingles to roofs.

10

Construction workers use big machines. They drive bulldozers to move dirt. Cranes lift heavy supplies to high places.

Clothes and Tools

Construction workers use many tools. They use saws to cut and shovels to dig. A tool belt holds a hammer, nails, and tape measure.

Construction workers wear special clothing to keep them safe. Hard hats protect their heads from falling objects.

Other clothing is important too. Safety glasses keep dirt and debris out of eyes. Thick gloves and heavy boots protect hands and feet.

18

Taking Things Down

Some construction crews take down old buildings. Workers smash walls with a wrecking ball. Excavators take away huge pieces.

Construction Workers Help

Construction workers build new buildings and roads. Construction workers help communities grow.

Glossary

architect—a person who designs and draws plans for buildings, bridges, and other construction projects

community—a group of people who live in the same area

debris—the scattered pieces of something that has been broken or destroyed

engineer—a person who uses science and math to plan, design, or build

excavator—a machine used to dig in the earth

skyscraper—a very tall building made of steel, concrete, and glass

Read More

Heos, Bridget. *Let's Meet a Construction Worker.* Community Helpers. Minneapolis: Millbrook Press, 2013.

McGill, Jordan. *Buildings.* Community Helpers. New York: AV2 by Weigl, 2012.

Troupe, Thomas Kingsley. *Knock It Down!* Destruction. North Mankato, Minn.: Capstone Press, 2014.

Internet Sites

FactHound offers a safe, fun way to find Internet sites related to this book. All of the sites on FactHound have been researched by our staff.

Here's all you do:

Visit *www.facthound.com*

Type in this code: 9781476539508

Super-cool stuff!

Check out projects, games and lots more at
www.capstonekids.com

Index

Word Count: 171
Grade: 1
Early-Intervention Level: 20

Editorial Credits
Erika L. Shores, editor; Gene Bentdahl, designer; Charmaine Whitman,
production specialist

Photo Credits
Capstone Studio: Karon Dubke, cover, 6, 8, 20; Dreamstime: Chaloemkiad, 4,
Dpproductions, 14; Glow Images: Flirt/Corbis/Curtis/Strauss, 12;
Shutterstock: ivvv1975, 10, Jaroslaw2313, 16, JMiks, 18